A New True Book

BOLIVIA

By Karen Jacobsen

Flag of Bolivia

CHILDRENS PRESS®
CHICAGO

A mother and son walk
with their cows on Bolivia's
high plateau.

PHOTO CREDITS

J984
JACOBSEN

AP/Wide World Photos, Inc.—31, 33 (right)

© Cameramann International, Ltd.—2, 40, 41 (left),
45 (left)

© Victor Englebert—6, 10, 15, 36, 37, 39

Historical Pictures Service—25 (bottom), 28

Journalism Services—© Antonio Suarez, 8, 18
(right), 42 (right)

Marion and Tony Morrison/South American
Pictures—© Tony Morrison, 9, 14, 17 (right), 23, 42
(left); © Marion Morrison, 13 (left); © Kimball
Morrison, 27

Odyssey/Frerck/Chicago—© Robert Frerck, 21
(2 photos)

Chip and Rosa Maria de la Cueva Peterson—12, 41
(right), 45 (right)

Photri—43

© Carl Purcell—44 (bottom)

Root Resources—© Anthony Mercierca, 13 (center);
© Kenneth W. Fink, 13 (right); © Ruth Welty, 35
(right)

SuperStock International, Inc.—35 (left); © Hubertus
Kanus, 6 (right), 25 (top), 33 (left), 44 (top); © Kurt
Scholz, 16 (left); © Antoinette Jongen, 16 (right);
© Shaw McCutcheon, 22

Tony Stone Worldwide/Chicago Ltd.—© Elizabeth
Harris, Cover; © Bill Staley, 7

Valan—© Jean-Marie Jro, 17 (left), 18 (left)

COVER: Child strapped on mother's back

Library of Congress Cataloging-in-Publication Data

Jacobsen, Karen.
   Bolivia / by Karen Jacobsen.
      p.   cm. — (A New true book)
   Includes index.
   Summary: Explores the geography, history, and
people of Bolivia.
   ISBN 0-516-01122-7
   1. Bolivia—Juvenile literature.   [1.   Bolivia.]
I. Title.
F3308.5.J33   1991   91-8889
984—dc20   CIP
                                                         AC

TABLE OF CONTENTS

THE NATION

Bolivia is the fifth largest country in South America. It is near the equator.

Five countries share borders with Bolivia—Peru, Brazil, Paraguay, Argentina, and Chile. Bolivia does not have a coastline.

Bolivia is a republic. It has a constitution, a president, and a Congress. The Congress makes Bolivia's laws.

There are almost 7

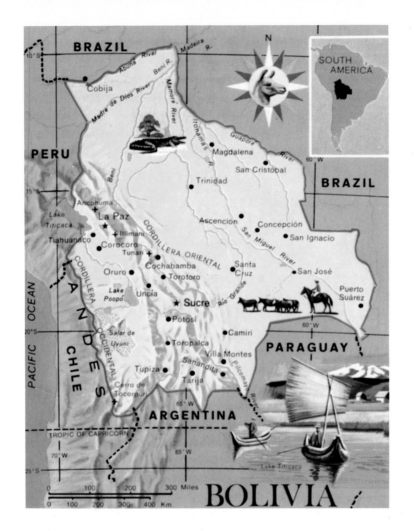

million people in Bolivia. The official language is Spanish. But the Indians of Bolivia speak their own languages.

Sucre (above) has many old buildings. The modern city of La Paz (right), at almost 12,000 feet, is the highest city in the world.

By law, the capital of Bolivia is the old city of Sucre. But the Congress holds its meetings in La Paz, Bolivia's largest and most modern city.

6

THE LAND

The Andes
Mountains run from
north to south
along the western
edge of South
America. In Bolivia,
the Andes split
into two parts—a
western range and
an eastern range.

A large plateau
lies between these

Many of Bolivia's
mountains are more than
20,000 feet high.

The Altiplano plateau is more than two miles high.

two ranges. It is 500 miles
long, and 80 to 100
miles wide. The plateau is
called the Altiplano. (In
Spanish, *alti* means "high,"
and *plano* means "flatland.")

The weather on the Altiplano is cool, dry, and windy. Crops will grow there, but not trees.

Lake Titicaca lies on the border between Bolivia and Peru. It is the largest lake in South America.

The Indians weave reeds into small boats called *balsas*. They use the boats to fish and to travel on Lake Titicaca.

The Yungas lie below the misty mountain peaks.

The Yungas are steep, narrow mountain valleys on the northeastern edge of the Andes Highlands. The valley floors have rich soil and are watered by streams from the mountains. Coffee, fruit trees, and other crops grow very well in the Yungas.

Thick, green rain forests grow on the mountainsides above the valleys.

The Valles is an area of broad valleys and rolling hills on the southeastern edge of the Andes Highlands. There are two kinds of soil in the Valles.

Near the mountains, the soil is hard and rocky. A tough, dry grass grows there. This land is used for grazing animals.

In the valleys, the soil is good for crops. Most of

A farm in the Oriente

Bolivia's food is grown
here on large farms.

The Oriente is a lowland
area. It covers more than
60 percent of eastern
Bolivia. In Spanish, *oriente*
means "the east."

The northern Oriente has
tropical forests, swamps,

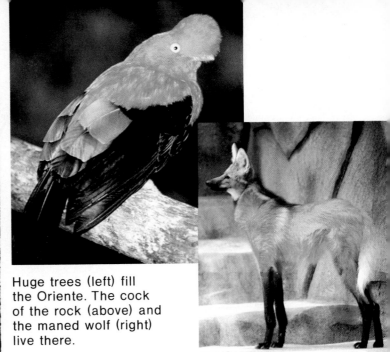

Huge trees (left) fill
the Oriente. The cock
of the rock (above) and
the maned wolf (right)
live there.

and many large rivers. It is
a wet, untamed place
filled with tall trees and
exotic plants and animals.
Few people live there.

The southern Oriente is
a land of woods and
grasslands. Cattle graze in
wide, open fields. There

Grasslands of the Gran Chaco

are also rice, tobacco, corn, and sugarcane plantations.

In the far south is a hot, dry area called the Gran Chaco. Only cactus and dry grasses grow there. The Gran Chaco spreads into Paraguay and Argentina.

A woman breaks up ore from the Cerro Rico.

RESOURCES

Bolivia has deposits of oil, natural gas, iron, and other minerals. These resources are sold to other countries.

In colonial days, silver was sold, too. But in the

late 1800s, the supply of silver was almost gone.

Since the 1900s Bolivia has sold the world tin—to make cans, automobiles, and other products. Tin mining is now Bolivia's biggest industry.

Tin miners (left) in Bolivia. The ore is carried from the mine in cars that run on tracks (right).

Hats of all shapes and sizes are worn by the Quechua Indians. Different styles show what village the wearer comes from.

THE PEOPLE

More than half of Bolivia's people are Indians. There are two main tribes. The Quechua live mainly in southern Bolivia, near the cities of Cochabamba and Sucre.

17

Aymara women (left) wear round felt hats and brightly colored skirts.
Altiplano men wear knit hats with earflaps (right).

The Aymara live near Lake
Titicaca on the Altiplano.
Many of Bolivia's Indians
live as farmers, hunters,
and gatherers. Most of
them are poor.

For four hundred years, people from Europe— especially from Spain— have been coming to Bolivia. Today, about 14 percent of the Bolivian people are European. They own most of the country's land and businesses.

About 30 percent of all Bolivians are mestizos. They are part European and part Indian. Many mestizos have jobs in the government and business.

LONG AGO IN BOLIVIA

People have lived on the Altiplano for about ten thousand years. At first, the people were wandering hunters. But after thousands of years, they learned to grow potatoes and grain. They raised animals. They were able to live in one place year after year.

By about the year A.D. 100, the people of the Altiplano had created a

At Tiahuanaco, huge stone blocks were cut to fit exactly in place. Many of the stones were covered with carvings. No one knows how the ancient people were able to make the buildings.

great civilization. At their city of Tiahuanaco, near Lake Titicaca, they built some amazing stone buildings.

21

THE INCAS

Around A.D. 1300, the Aymara tribe ruled over the Altiplano. Then, in the 1400s, the Incas of Peru came south and defeated the Aymara. The Altiplano

The Incas built terraces, or steps, in the hillsides to raise crops. These terraces are still used today.

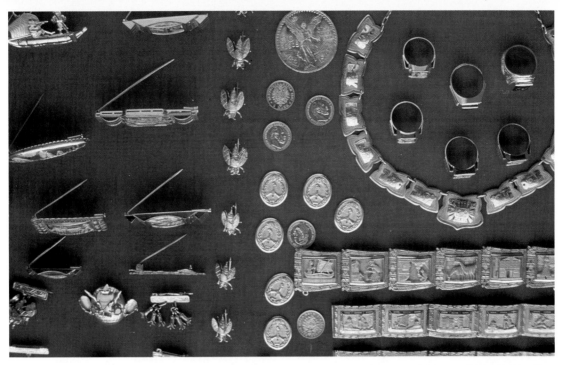
Examples of gold jewelry made by artists in La Paz

and all its people became
part of the great Inca
Empire.

There was great wealth
in the Inca Empire. Skilled
craft workers turned gold
and silver into beautiful
jewelry and other objects. **23**

SPANISH RULE

In the 1500s, Spanish soldiers arrived in South America. They searched for gold and silver. They took treasure and land away from the native peoples.

In 1533, the Spanish adventurer Francisco Pizarro killed the Inca emperor in Peru. Pizarro took over the Inca Empire. He sent Diego de Almagro to the Altiplano to find gold and silver and to rule

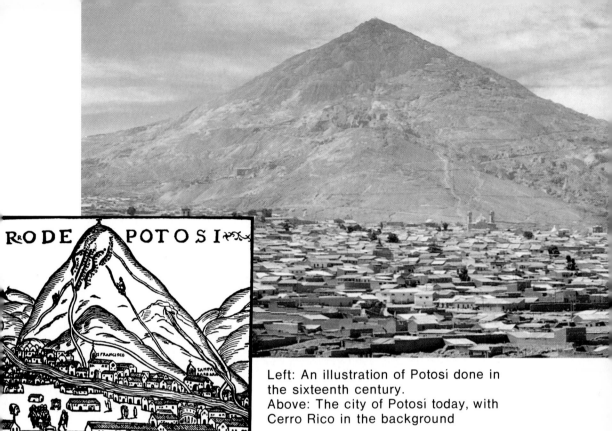

Left: An illustration of Potosi done in
the sixteenth century.
Above: The city of Potosi today, with
Cerro Rico in the background

over the Indians. In 1545,
the Spanish discovered the
Cerro Rico—"rich hill"—at
Potosí. This was one of
the largest deposits of
silver ore ever found in
one place.

During the 1600s and 1700s, the Spanish kings sent men called viceroys to govern their Spanish colonies. The viceroys made laws and collected taxes. Spanish soldiers made people obey the laws and pay the taxes.

But many people in the colonies did not like paying taxes to a faraway king. They wanted independence from Spain.

Simón Bolívar

INDEPENDENCE

In the 1820s, the
Spanish colonists formed
an army. Its leader was
Simón Bolívar of
Venezuela. Bolívar sent
General Antonio José de
Sucre and his soldiers to

27

General Sucre was
Bolivia's first president.

attack the Spanish army in
Peru. In 1825, Sucre's army
defeated the Spanish. Peru
was free from Spain.

Bolívar and the generals
divided Peru into two
nations. The northern part
kept the name Peru, and
the southern part was
named Bolivia to honor
General Bolívar.

LOST LAND

In 1828, Peru decided to attack and capture Bolivia. The fighting lasted for several years. Finally, the two countries made peace. They agreed to work together as partners.

But Chile did not want them to be partners. In 1839, Chile's army invaded Bolivia and forced an end to the agreement.

In 1879, Chile's army invaded Bolivia again. After

four years of fighting, Bolivia lost the war and was forced to give all of its land on the Pacific Ocean to Chile.

Then, in 1902 and 1903, Bolivia gave up more land. Brazil got two large pieces of the Oriente—without a fight.

In the 1930s, Bolivia had to give up another large piece of land to Paraguay. In a little over one hundred years, Bolivia had lost almost half of its land.

MANY GOVERNMENTS

Victor Paz Estenssoro
was the leader
of the MNR party.

Between 1825 and 1952 Bolivia changed its government and leaders more than one hundred times—usually by force.

In 1952, the National Revolutionary Movement (MNR) came into power.

31

It wanted to improve the lives of Bolivia's poor miners and farmers.

The MNR stayed in power until 1964. Then a group of army officers took over by force. They put an end to the MNR and its changes.

In 1982, the Congress was allowed to elect a president. They chose Hernán Siles Zuazo.

In 1985, Víctor Paz Estenssoro was elected

The Legislative Palace in La Paz (left) and President Jaime Paz Zamora

president. (He had been MNR president in 1952.) President Paz Estenssoro made many improvements and put strong rules in place. In 1989, Jaime Paz Zamora became Bolivia's new president.

TODAY IN BOLIVIA

Some Bolivians are very wealthy. Their homes are big, with walled gardens. Other Europeans and mestizos often live in modern houses with electricity and running water. But most Bolivians live in small houses near the cities and towns.

The Indians on the Altiplano build one-room houses of adobe.

Left: Houses made of bamboo and
palm leaves   Right: Adobe houses
with thatched roofs

   In the Oriente, the forest
people build their houses
of bamboo poles with
palm-leaf roofs.

   The Altiplano Indians
wear handwoven clothing
made from the wool of
llamas or alpacas. The

Bolivian women use their shawls to carry everything from food to babies.

women wear brightly colored shawls called *aquayos*.

On market day people from the countryside go into the nearby towns. All kinds of Bolivian foods are for sale at the markets.

Vegetables for sale at a market in Potosi

The most common are oca
(a kind of potato), corn,
and quinoa (a kind of
grain).

For the very poor people
of Bolivia, life is hard.
They do not have jobs.
They do not have safe

37

water to drink. They must spend all their time trying to get enough food to stay alive.

The Bolivian government is trying to find ways to help its poor people. It is teaching people how to keep their drinking water clean. It is helping people to start new businesses to employ more workers.

EDUCATION

In Bolivia, less than 75 percent of the people can read and write. The government has started special classes to teach reading to adults.

Education is free for all children from age 7 to 14.

Many schools do not have enough money to buy books, pencils, and paper.

A mathematics class in a teachers' college

In primary school, students learn reading, writing, and other basic subjects.

Some students go to private schools. They offer more subjects and prepare students for further education.

In the past, only a few Bolivian children ever went to high school. But now there are more teachers and public high schools.

The major cities have government universities. There are three private universities in Bolivia.

Left: The University of San Andrés.
Below: The courtyard of the University of Chuquisaca in Sucre

RECREATION

Soccer is the favorite sport in Bolivia. It is played by professional teams and by schoolchildren. Festivals, weddings, and birthday parties are special days. The Bolivians listen

Carnival celebrations are held before Lent. The devil masks (below) represent an evil spirit who is believed to live in the center of the earth. The eyes are made from light bulbs.

Young
Bolivian
musicians

to music played on flutes
and stringed instruments.

Most Bolivians are
Roman Catholics. They
celebrate religious holidays.
Carnival—before Lent—is
a special time for parties,
costumes, dancing, and
parades.

La Paz lies at the
foot of Mount Illimani.
The waters of Lake
Titicaca (left) are
very cold and deep.

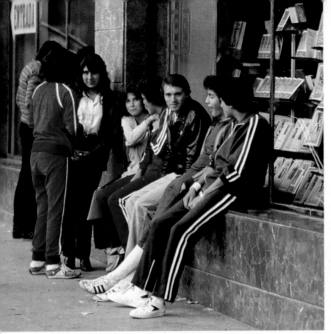

La Paz University students (left) talk in front of a bookstore.
An Aymara Indian (right) at the market in La Paz

Bolivia is a land of great natural beauty. But it is also a land of many hardships. Its people are working to find ways to improve their lives. They are trying to make Bolivia into a strong, independent, and modern nation.

WORDS YOU SHOULD KNOW

aquayo (uh • KYE • oh) — a brightly colored shawl worn by the women of Bolivia

cactus (KACK • tiss) — a plant that grows in desert areas. It has thick stems covered with needlelike spines.

civilization (sih • vih • lih • ZAY • shun) — a society that has developed government, arts and sciences, and cities

constitution (kahn • stih • TOO • shun) — a system of basic laws or rules for the government of a country

deposit (dih • PAH • zit) — something left in the ground, such as rocks or minerals, by the action of the forces of nature

equator (ih • KWAY • ter) — an imaginary line around the earth, equally distant from the North and South poles

exotic (ex • AH • tick) — strange; different

hardship (HARD • ship) — difficulty; trouble; suffering

independence (in • dih • PEN • dins) — freedom from control by another country or person

mestizos (meh • TEE • zohz) — people who are partly Indian and partly European

minerals (MIN • er • ilz) — useful substances such as iron ore or diamonds that are found in the ground

oca (O • kah) — a plant that is like a potato

Oriente (or • ee • EN • tay) — a division of Bolivia; the name means "the east."

plateau (plat • OH) — an area of elevated flat land

quinoa (kee • NO • ah) — a kind of grain grown in Bolivia

republic (rih • PUB • lick) — a country with elected leaders

revolutionary (reh • vil • OO • shun • ary) — working for changes in government or in society

sugarcane (SHOOG • er • kain) — a plant that is grown for the sugar contained in the stems

swamp (SWAHMP) — an area of low-lying land in which water collects; wetland

treasure (TREZJ•er) —gold, silver, precious stones, or other valuable items

tropical (TRAH•pih•kil) —of the warm, humid areas near the equator

viceroy (VICE•roy) —a person who rules a colony in the name of a king; a governor

INDEX

About the Author

Karen Jacobsen is a graduate of the University of Connecticut and Syracuse University. She has been a teacher and is a writer. She likes to find out about interesting subjects and then write about them.